WELCOME TO

GRAND TETON

NATIONAL PARK

BY MARYBETH LORBIECKI

Content Consultant: Andrew White, Assistant Public Affairs Officer, Grand Teton National Park

MAP KEY

The maps throughout this
book use the following icons:

 Bear Viewing Area

 Campground

 Driving Excursion

 Elk Viewing Area

 Hiking Trail

 Lodging

 Marmot Viewing Area

 Point of Interest

 Ranger Station

 Visitor Center

 Wildflower Area

 Wooded Area

About National Parks

A national park is an area of land that has been set aside by Congress. National parks protect nature and history. In most cases, no hunting, grazing, or farming is allowed. The first national park in the United States—and in the world—was Yellowstone National Park. It is located in parts of Wyoming, Idaho, and Montana. It was founded in 1872. In 1916, the U.S. National Park Service began.

Today, the National Park Service manages more than 415 sites. Some of these sites are historic, such as the Statue of Liberty or the Martin Luther King Jr. National Historic Site. Other park areas preserve wild land. The National Park Service manages 40% of the nation's wilderness areas, including national parks. Each year, millions of people from around the world visit these national parks. Visitors may camp, go canoeing, or go for a hike. Or, they may simply sit and enjoy the scenery, wildlife, and the quiet of the land.

TABLE OF

The Child's World®
childsworld.com

Published by The Child's World®
1980 Lookout Drive
Mankato, MN 56003-1705
800-599-READ • www.childsworld.com

ISBN
9781503823426

LCCN
2017944749

Cartographer
Matt Kania/Map Hero, Inc.

Photo Credits
Ariel Celeste Photography/Shutterstock.com: 13; Clarence
Upchurch/Shutterstock.com: cover, 4; F11photo/Dreamstime:
18; Green Mountain Exposure/Shutterstock.com: 23; IrinaK/
Shutterstock.com: 19, 24-25; JeffGoulden/iStockphoto.
com: 16; Jeffrey T. Kreulen/Shutterstock.com: 15; Jess Kraft/
Shutterstock.com: 7; Kan Kankavee/Shutterstock.com: 12; Nagel
Photography/Shutterstock.com: 21; Pung/Shutterstock.com: 1,
2-3; Tom Olson/Shutterstock.com: 9; Tom Tietz/Shutterstock.com:
11; William Michael Norton/Dreamstime: 26

On the cover and this page
Grand Teton National Park is one of the
most beautiful places on Earth, especially at
sunrise.

On page 1
Grand Teton is the tallest peak in the park. At
13,770 feet (4,197 m), the peak is sometimes
covered by wispy clouds.

On pages 2–3
The views along the Snake River are some of
the most beautiful in the park.

Printed in the United States of America
PA02357

WELCOME TO
GRAND TETON NATIONAL PARK

CONTENTS

A Slice of the Wild West

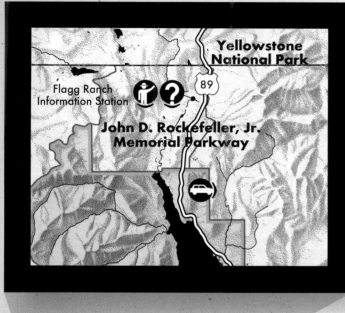

Welcome to Grand Teton National Park! You're in the western state of Wyoming. Look at those beautiful mountains! The Tetons are the youngest and most rugged peaks in the Rocky Mountains.

Grand Teton National Park sits in the largest patch of wild lands in America, (other than Alaska). This area is known as the Greater Yellowstone **Ecosystem**. This natural community is about the size of West Virginia. This area includes Grand Teton and Yellowstone National Parks, three national wildlife refuges, and six national forests and **wilderness areas**. The animals move from one area to another. So do visitors. The two national parks are connected by the John D. Rockefeller, Jr. Memorial Parkway.

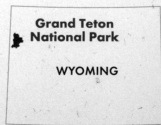

Grand Teton National Park

WYOMING

The Teton Park Road runs along the base of the Tetons. It offers close-up views of the mountains and scenic stops where you can take a photograph or look for wildlife.

Walk on the Wild Side

Head to Jenny Lake Visitor Center, and see the sparkling blue-green water of glacial Jenny Lake. Thousands of years ago, large sheets of moving ice called **glaciers** carved the **canyons** of the Teton Mountains. When the ice melted, lakes were left on the valley floor. The glistening blue water is especially clear. Jenny Lake is too cold and too deep for most water plants to grow.

At the dock, a shuttle boat awaits you for a trip to Hidden Falls. Climb aboard! A boat captain will give you an introduction to this amazing place. Once you've crossed the lake, prepare to hike. The trail winds its way to the falls. If you've packed water and snacks, go all the way to Inspiration Point. From there, you can look down across the valley below. If you are really adventurous, keep hiking. Stop and have lunch along the way. You'll get a view of the stunning **Cascade** Canyon. Keep your eyes alert! You may see a pika, a yellow-bellied marmot, or even a moose.

Reminders of the Ice Age

Some signs of the last Ice Age can still be seen. Look at the snowy areas that decorate the park's peaks. The snow is there even in the summer. Many of these areas are glaciers. Glaciers are rivers of ice that flow slowly downhill.

Jenny Lake is the second largest lake in the park (the largest lake is Jackson Lake). Visitors often rent boats to use on the calm waters.

A Hike to Alaska

When you hike in the Tetons, many trails go from the valley to a much higher area. It's like climbing from Colorado to Alaska. You go through five different nature communities that are based on weather, soil, and water. They are sagebrush **flats**, wet meadows, rivers and lakes, spruce and pine forests, and **alpine** meadows. Each area is a small ecosystem, and in each one you'll see different plants and wildlife.

You'll find sagebrush flats on the dry valley floor. Sage, grasses, and wildflowers carpet the ground. You may see bison, pronghorn antelope, ground squirrels, coyotes, and badgers. Sage grouse, meadowlarks, and red-tailed hawks can also be seen. If you're lucky, you may even spot a wolf.

A lone bison grazes in a meadow near Grand Teton. This picture shows some of the different nature communities found in the park. The bison is grazing on the sagebrush flats. Behind the bison, you can see a forest. Another forest grows farther in the distance, stopping about halfway up the mountain.

11

🚶🚶 The Snake River flows through the southern part of Yellowstone National Park before entering Grand Teton National Park. The river enters Jackson Lake, passes through Jackson Lake Dam, and then winds its way slowly through the rest of the park.

In some areas along the trail are low spots where water gathers. These are the wet meadows. Willows provide shade. Plenty of small animals such as water-loving snakes, frogs, lizards, and salamanders dart, hop, swim, and slither here. Moose gorge on willows and water plants.

The park's rivers, lakes, and marshes offer homes to many creatures. Birds warble around gleaming glacial lakes. Ducks land noisily on marshes. Trout glide along in the Snake River as otters pounce and play. Eagles soar overhead, and osprey dive. Visitors can raft, canoe, and swim.

Look toward the skyline to see towering lodgepole pine, fir, and spruce. These are the high forests. Trees in these cool forests clean the air. They give off a fresh, pungent scent. Elk munch on grass, while mule deer feast on tree bark and seedlings. Black bear waddle around in search of roots, berries, and bugs.

Stay Back from Animals

The animals in the park might seem tame, but they are not. Give wildlife a lot of space, or they get frightened. Don't ever come up to a wild animal, not even for a photo. Always stay away from their young, too. Wild animals don't like humans going near their babies.

Bear Safety

Here are some tips to help you stay safe in bear country.

- Make noise. Sing, whistle, or talk as you hike. If bears know you're nearby, they will avoid you!
- Be alert. If you see fresh tracks or bear poop, hike somewhere else.
- Stay far away. If you spot a bear, give it lots of space.
- Store all food in bear-resistant containers. Never keep food in your tent!

Up in the highest lands, beyond most trees, you will see more rock and less soil. These are the alpine meadows. Be careful to stay on the trail, because the plants up here are fragile. Lichens cover the rocks. The few trees in this area are small and twisted. Many of them are hundreds of years old. Wildflowers display their vivid colors. Bighorn sheep ramble. Cold winds whistle and snow is never far away.

Like other higher areas in the Tetons, this mountain meadow near Amphitheater Lake is carpeted with wildflowers.

Native Americans began using the valley known as Jackson Hole 11,000 years ago. They lived and hunted in the area, as well as held religious ceremonies. Jackson Hole was named for Davey Jackson, an 1800s fur trader who was one of the founders of the Rocky Mountain Fur Company.

Down to Jackson Hole

Fur trappers named any valley surrounded by mountains or cliffs a "hole." Jackson Hole was a favorite place for native peoples. Here they hunted animals and gathered plants. Jackson Hole remains a beloved place for the Shoshone and other nations. These mountains have long been a place for them to make "vision quests." They pray and seek guidance about their life and their people. Some native spiritual leaders believe the Tetons are the hub of a Medicine Wheel of holy sites across America.

Hole Up in Jackson

The nearby town of Jackson is full of Old West history. Clomp down the wooden sidewalks. Watch the nightly gun fight, or hoot and holler at the rodeo. Go ahead and experience some of the other fun things to do in this Wild West town.

The valley was named Jackson's Hole after Davey Jackson. He was a fur trader who trapped animals for their fur here in 1829. Eventually, the name was shortened. Ranchers began to follow the fur traders. The ranchers brought cattle. At Menor's Ferry, you can still see a general store, an old cabin, and the rebuilt ferryboat of homesteader Bill Menor. He lived here in the 1890s and early 1900s.

Bill Menor was one of the first settlers in the Jackson Hole area. Soon after arriving in 1892, Menor built several buildings along the Snake River. He then built a ferry (a flat raft) that carried people, goods, and horses across the river. The settlement of Menor's Ferry is near the present-day village of Moose, Wyoming.

A Long View through History

The Old West isn't really very old around here! For a look back in time, go to Colter Bay. Take a hike on the Hermitage Point Trail. Choose the left fork that turns for Swan Lake. This scenic trail will bring you by the lake. Climb a small hill, and you'll get a terrific view of Mount Moran.

Staring at Mount Moran and Swan Lake, you can imagine the extreme history of this land. Not far from your feet lies an earthquake **fault**. This crack in the **Earth's crust** runs along the base of the Tetons. Millions of years ago, earthquakes shifted the land along this fault line. Mountains of **granite** and **gneiss** rose into the sky. The valley was created. Then came a long period in which the land was covered by glaciers. They melted, and wild plants sprouted. Soon, animals arrived. Finally, people came! Earthquakes and glaciers continue to form this area today.

Indian Life

On your way back to the modern age, stop at the Colter Bay Visitor Center. You'll learn so much more about the park and its history. See objects made and used by the many Native Americans who once lived here.

Mount Moran seems to sparkle as the sun begins to rise. The mountain isn't as tall as Grand Teton, but at 12,605 feet (3,842 m), it's still very impressive. Mount Moran is named for Thomas Moran, who was a famous landscape artist in the late 1800s.

Adventurous Science

I f you don't have a snow parka, the best months to visit are July and August. It's sunny, warm, and jam-packed with things to do. Watch the wildlife. Take a raft trip on the Snake River. Go horseback riding. Enjoy a long hike, perhaps even a stargazing walk at night. Go canoeing, fishing, backpacking, or rock climbing. Then be sure to rest your feet by a crackling fire. Stare up into a night bursting with stars.

The Exum Ridge is a favorite place for mountain climbers to test their skills. The Ridge is divided into two parts: the upper and the lower. The ridge was named after mountaineer Glenn Exum, who was the first to climb it in 1931.

May, September, and October are usually still warm enough to enjoy the area. In winter, activities change. Snowshoeing, cross-country skiing, and ice fishing are all options at this time of year. And that's just the beginning.

Don't miss the Junior Ranger program. If you are here for a long visit, check out the Teton Science School. That's where kids work with scientists to study this great "land" laboratory—the Greater Yellowstone Ecosystem. There are week-long programs for students in third through eighth grade. There are also family and teacher workshops. Programs for high school and college students are available, too. Everyone gets a chance to study nature in the wild outdoors.

The Science Laboratories

Research is always going on in the Greater Yellowstone Ecosystem. Some subjects being studied now include the migration path of mule deer, fish and water ecosystems, the relationship between red foxes and people, how fire affects the wild plant and animal communities, and the ways of elk and grizzlies.

Enjoy incredible views while cross-country skiing in Grand Teton National Park.

🚶🚶 "The Old Patriarch" is another one of the park's treasures. This very old limber pine tree was struck by lightning many years ago. The strike seared off part of the tree's main branches, leaving it with its gnarly look. The Old Patriarch and its meadow is one of the most photographed spots in the park.

The Gift of a Park

Having now explored this place, you can understand why it is so treasured. John D. Rockefeller, Jr. loved the Teton country, too. He bought and donated more than 33,000 acres (13,355 hectares) to the park. This gift expanded the original Grand Teton National Park. The 24,000-acre (9,712-hectare) John D. Rockefeller, Jr. Memorial Parkway links Grand Teton and Yellowstone national parks and was named in his honor.

Now it's up to all of us to take care of this park. It's our job to preserve its ecosystems. Then we can pass it on as a gift to everyone who comes after us.

Yellowstone National Park

Flagg Ranch Information Station

89

John D. Rockefeller, Jr. Memorial Parkway

Grand Teton National Park

WYOMING

NORTH

0   4 Miles

Grand Teton National Park

Colter Bay Visitor Center

Indian Arts Museum

Jackson Lake

Hermitage Point Trail

Mount Moran

Inspiration Point

Hidden Falls

Cascade Canyon

Jenny Lake Visitor Center

Jenny Lake

26

Jackson Hole   Snake River

191

Bridger-Teton National Forest

Caribou-Targhee National Forest

Grand Teton

Menor's Ferry

Sagebrush Flats

Craig Thomas Discovery and Visitor Center

Snake River

to town of Jackson

GRAND TETON NATIONAL PARK FAST FACTS

Date founded: Original park, 1929; expanded in 1950

Location: Western Wyoming

Size: 485 square miles (1,256 sq km); 310,400 acres (125,614 hectares)

Major habitats: Sagebrush flats, wet meadows, rivers and lakes, spruce and pine forests, and alpine meadows

Important landforms: Peaks, glaciers, Snake River, Jackson Lake

Elevation:
    Highest: 13,770 feet (4,197 m) at Grand Teton
    Lowest: 6,350 feet (1,935 m) at the park's south boundary

Weather:
    Average yearly rainfall: 10 inches (25 cm)
    Average yearly snowfall: 191 inches (485 cm)
    Hottest temperature: 93 F (34 C)
    Coolest temperature: -63 F (-53 C) in Moran

Number of animal species: 17 species of carnivores, 6 species of hoofed animals, 22 species of rodents, 16 species of fish, 4 species of reptiles, and more than 300 species of birds

Number of plant species: 7 species of conifer trees and more than 900 species of flowering plants

Number of endangered or threatened animal species: 3

Native people: There are more than 20 affiliated tribes, including the Shoshone, Gros Ventre, Flathead, Blackfoot, Crow, and Nez Perce

Number of visitors each year: Almost 5 million

Important sites and landmarks: Major peaks, the Snake River and its tributaries, seven glacial lakes, 230 miles (370 km) of hiking trails, historic Menor's Ferry, pioneer/ranch buildings, and Jackson Lake Dam

Tourist activities: Wildlife watching in five different natural communities, climbing, rafting, canoeing, fishing, horseback riding, and photography

GLOSSARY

alpine (AL-pine): An area of land so high that it is above the place where trees grow easily is called alpine. The alpine areas in Grand Teton National Park have only a few wind-twisted trees because it is too cold and dry for most trees.

canyons (KAN-yunz): Deep, narrow valleys surrounded by cliffs are called canyons. Grand Teton National Park has several canyons.

cascade (kass-KAYD): A steep, rushing fall of water that drops from level to level is called a cascade. Grand Teton National Park has a trail that leads to a canyon with a cascading waterfall in it.

Earth's crust (ERTHS KRUST): The thick layer of hardened rock covering the inner core of the planet is called the Earth's crust. A crack in this crust lies under the park, and it caused the earthquakes that pushed up the peaks.

ecosystem (EE-koh-sis-tum): A community of plants and animals that depend on each other and share the same weather and water systems is an ecosystem. Grand Teton National Park has five different ecosytems.

fault (FALT): A crack in the crust of the planet is called a fault. The earthquakes that happened thousands of years ago in the park happened along a fault line.

flats (FLATS): The plains, or low, flat spots of the valley floor, are called flats. The flats in Grand Teton National Park are known for the sagebrush growing in them.

glaciers (GLAY-shurz): Huge masses of slow-moving ice are glaciers. The peaks in Grand Teton National Park have glaciers on them.

gneiss (NICE): Gneiss is a very hard rock that is mixed and melted like granite but also contains crushed bits of long-dead plants and animals. Grand Teton's peaks also have gneiss in them.

granite (GRAN-it): Granite is a very hard rock formed of crystals (such as quartz) and minerals molten together in the hot areas of the Earth's core. Grand Teton's peaks have granite in them.

wilderness areas (WIL-der-ness AYR-ee-uz): A large area of wild, natural land without human-made buildings and roads is called a wilderness area. There are three areas protected as wilderness around Grand Teton National Park: Vinegar Hole Wilderness, Jedediah Smith Wilderness, and the Teton Wilderness.

TO FIND OUT MORE

Λ

FURTHER READING

Craighead, Shirley A.
Bugling Elk and Sleeping Grizzlies: The Who, What, and When of Yellowstone and Grand Teton National Parks.
Guilford, CT: Globe Pequot Press, 2004.

Frisch, Nate.
Grand Teton National Park: Preserving America.
Mankato, MN: Creative Paperbacks, 2016

Graf, Mike.
Grand Teton National Park: To the Top of the Grand.
Guilford, CT: FalconGuides, 2013.

ON THE WEB

Visit our home page for lots of links
about Grand Teton National Park:

childsworld.com/links

NOTE TO PARENTS, TEACHERS, AND LIBRARIANS:
*We routinely check our Web links to make sure they're safe, active sites—
so encourage your readers to check them out!*

INDEX